D0877171

INSIDE THE MIND
OF AN ANGRY MAN

Inside the Mind of an Angry Man

Evan L. Katz, M.C., LPC

Copyright © 2012 by Evan L. Katz

Brighton Publishing
555 Sun Valley Drive
Suite B-1
Roswell, GA 30076

www.angerguy.com

ISBN: 978-0-578-09728-2

All rights reserved. No part of this publication may be reproduced, stored in a retrieval system or transmitted, in any form, or by any means, electronic, mechanical, recorded, photocopied, or otherwise, without the prior written permission of both the copyright owner and the above publisher of this book, except by a reviewer who may quote brief passages in a review.

The scanning, uploading, and distribution of this book via the Internet or via any other means without the permission of the publisher is illegal and punishable by law. Please purchase only authorized electronic editions and do not participate in or encourage electronic piracy of copyrightable materials. Your support of the author's rights is appreciated.

Printed in the United States of America

For my beautiful daughter
Sarah Rebekah

And for my wonderful Mom

And for you too Dad...
just because.

CONTENTS

EVAN'S STORY 17

WHY YOU NEED THIS BOOK.............................31

WHO IS THE ANGRY MAN? 35

THREE TYPES OF ANGRY MEN 43
    The Aggressive Type 43
    The Passive Type 46
    The Passive-Aggressive Type.............................49

THE ANGER CYCLE...53
    Self-Image 54
    Distorted Perceptions 58
    Defense Mechanisms **60**

THE ANGER SHIELD 65

THE 5 "A"S OF ANGER 73
    Action...74
    Awareness...75
    Acknowledgement 76
    Acceptance 77
    Amends 78

HOW TO CONTEND WITH AN ANGRY MAN ..79

COMMON QUESTIONS ABOUT ANGRY MEN ..83

FINAL THOUGHTS 93

Acknowledgements

My gratitude is endless. Without the support of so many, this book would have never been written. First and foremost, I thank my family. Mom, for her strength and unconditional love, my brother David and his wife Julia, for their support and encouragement, and my daughter Sarah and nieces Rayna and Hanna, for reminding me what living is really all about.

I appreciate so many of my friends and colleagues who have supported me in this venture. I'm grateful to the Bad Ass Melanoma Warriors Facebook group for helping me feel connected and reminding me to "live" and not just survive. To my dear friends of Bill W., without whom I could not have possibly accepted my malady, and to all my Facebook friends, thank you so much for your endless support and for being so selfless and unconditional. And finally, to George...my closest confidant, who sees the worst of me and accepts me anyhow. You are valued more than you know.

Sincere thanks to Gerald Hedlund, who met deadlines in spite of a hurricane ripping the roof off his home. To Jacki, Jonathan, Vince, and Michael, with Self Publishing, Inc., whose guidance, patience, and support have been invaluable. I would strongly recommend anyone writing a book to work with your company. To

Bevan, a teenage IT guru somewhere in South Africa, whose skill, reliability, and strong character have been a breath of fresh air, and to Cyndee Davis, whose talent I could not possibly have done without.

I made a commitment to myself to write this book as part of my recovery from cancer. I have tremendous gratitude to my physicians for giving me this opportunity, as they are responsible for saving my life. Anyone who thinks that doctors don't care hasn't met mine. They cared enough to insist that I transform into a stronger, wiser, and more useful human being. To my surgeon, Dr. Keith Delman at Emory University, for the work he did removing the tumor from my back, but more than that, for going out of his way to meet with my daughter and family and explain the challenges we were about to face. To the coolest oncologist on the planet, Dr. Daniel Dubovsky, who continues to empower me to be a partner in my recovery and not just a patient. And to his support team, who took the brunt of my rants during treatment yet continued to be nice to me anyhow. To Dr. George Wong, whose presence I try to model, and for his sincerity, advice, knowledge, and wisdom of both Western and Chinese medicine. His complex mixes of herbs continue to save my life. To my dermatologist, Dr. Russell Harris, an expert in skin cancer, who tells the most interesting stories each time he does another excision on my back, and to everyone in his office for always going the extra mile to take care of both my daughter and me. To Dr. Alan Miller, for not firing me as a patient even though I rarely follow his directions. To my mentor, Dr. Richard Blue, for telling me each time we meet, "YOU'RE THE MAN!" To Dr. Ray Horowitz, for keeping the chemicals in my head relatively straight since chemotherapy. And very special thanks to Dr. Susan Russell, for her knowledge and practice of acupuncture, her ongoing spiritual guidance, compassion, friendship, and vision, and for writing such a beautiful Foreword to this book.

And finally, to my clients...those I learn from the most. Thank you for your courage and fortitude, and for trusting me to help you. I'm humbled and privileged to be (or have been) an important part of your lives.

FOREWORD

Dr. Susan Russell holds a Ph.D of Energy Medicine
-Th.D of Holism L.Ac. (Licensed NCCAOM Board
Certified Acupuncturist) QiGong - LMSW
(Licensed Master of Social Work)
Turning Point Healing Center
Award Winner of the Best of Marietta
2009 & 2010 -Holistic Help Services
4343 Shallowford Rd. Ste. H-5
Marietta, GA 30062
770-552-4155
www.Turningpointhc.com

Anyone who is intrigued by *Inside the Mind of an Angry Man* is already interested in exploring new possibilities for dealing with anger...and healing from its devastating effects. By turning the pages of *Inside the Mind of an Angry Man*, you will learn how to turn your pages of anger into a new life chapter by shedding your old personal historical landscape and scripting new pages filled with your new "true-self norm."

Evan Katz offers an exciting, clearly written, candid look at anger, its realities, and its repercussions. His insights and understanding confirm that he is a knowledgeable authority not only on the subject of anger, but also on a clear path to personal transformation, one he has walked himself with tenacity and resolve.

Evan is able to cut through the murky waters of anger with plain language that is easily grasped by those wanting to learn more. He sheds light on the complexities and challenges posed by the condition of underlying latent rage in a world where anger and angry people are so often misunderstood. He is unusually gifted at being able to walk anyone through the dimly-lit world of anger and provides a proven map to cast off anger methodically for those who wrestle with their angry dragons.

This book is impressive. It is ideal for anyone who is in a relationship with an angry person, as well as the rest of us who understand that within us all lies a part that expresses or suppresses an anger that needs to be tamed and transformed. Practitioners will also be drawn by the book's simple depth of detail woven on every page. Evan's book not only discloses the challenges that he faced but provides a step by step understanding of the core issues that shape the world of anger and the way out of it.

Perhaps the most daunting challenge faced by anyone who has a desire to change his circumstances is facing himself. Like feuding polarized groups, ego aspects cling to old roles to retain control and thereby avoid feeling the devastation of shame and powerlessness. These imprints remain on replay as the result of early childhood experiences, when a child could not possibly overcome these states. Evan offers clear direction to shift from that frozen childhood state to an adult with self-dignity... capable of deeper, more meaningful intimacy with others. Anybody who has spent any time in Angry-ville will find familiar guideposts here.

For all of us who continue to self-explore and shed patterns that no longer serve, thank you, Evan, for the courage to give voice to your story and the stories of many others. The draft copy which Evan Katz sent me several weeks ago is already dog-eared from referencing use.

—Dr. Susan Russell

EVAN'S STORY

ANGER has always worked well for me. Of course, I learned from the best. My father was a dominating and domineering force to be reckoned with. On top of his enduring alcoholism and insidious anger, he was a criminal trial lawyer who knew how to win.

As the older of two boys, I was his favorite target, his emotional punching bag. He was a master of twisting arguments around to make me feel that I was lucky just to be alive. He knew all the right buttons to push and would browbeat my mom, brother, and me into darkness, fear, and submission. I grew to believe that someday, someone was going to find out that I was nothing more than the trash my father kept telling me I was and that I would be lucky just to be tolerated.

Perception is such an abstract thing, isn't it? When I was growing up, enduring the heartache of that childhood seemed normal to me. Like most children, I grew up believing what I was told. If I didn't accept what my father told me, then I was chastised. I came to believe that it wasn't my right to question and that my thoughts were worthless.

When I was a child, my father was God in my eyes. He modeled the behavior that I would eventually come to expect from the rest of the world.

By the time I was seven, I had grown to accept that I was not worthy of love, that I was simply no good. My father's rage left me believing that nothing I ever did was good enough for him. This left me feeling different and "less than" all the other kids. I had learned not only how to cope as a "nothing," but also that the goodness I felt as a human being, however thin and brief it may have been, was foolish. My focus was to somehow manage not to be discovered for the fraud I believed myself to be. Unbeknownst to me, I had become a master of deceit, hiding my fear, my pain, and my shame for just wanting to be me.

Once I'd reached age ten, I saw myself as nothing but an illusion. My primary focus when around others had become emotional safety. I had the fake smile down to a science. I was smart, and I used my intelligence to secure that safety. I began to master the ability to manipulate and navigate the world around me, to mold it the way I needed it to be molded and to build walls that hid the real me—the me that was unworthy of love, respect, and affection.

During my early teens, I was a maniac. I had become my father to my mother. She struggled to play peacemaker, just as she had done with him. And just like it was with him, it was with me: it didn't work. I was a tornado, ripping through her life and the lives of those closest to me, completely oblivious to the pain I felt...and to the pain I was causing them.

It was during these adolescent and early adult years that I began to convert the chaos and fear in my life into the need for control. I yelled, raged, punched holes in walls, and used defiance and verbal assaults to dominate others.

It was after I joined the military that I slipped into the world of alcohol. There, it was acceptable to act out my anger through alcohol, which I did quite well, eventually crossing that invisible line from "want" to "need." Alcohol was like magic to me, whisking away the feelings I had spent years working so hard to mask. It was dependable, because it always worked. And it was readily available. It became the only friend I really trusted.

I recall looking in the mirror one day. I was twenty-five. Completely spent from a tantrum of rage, I stood gazing at the stranger reflected back at me. I didn't see myself; I saw my father. I smiled, for whatever reason, but he didn't smile back. My life was a mess and even though I had become him, I still couldn't win his approval. I had come to hate myself and to believe with certainty that my fear of being fortunate enough to just be tolerated was deserved and true.

I was thirty-six when I received the call that my father had suffered a massive heart attack. It was the day before Thanksgiving. I had a family now and had developed a successful private practice as a psychotherapist. I had largely distanced myself from him, yet deep inside I still blamed my father for my outbursts of anger and ongoing turmoil in relationships.

Reluctantly, I made the trek to do what a son is supposed to do; be there and be supportive—even if I had to fake it. By the time I arrived, he had become stable but was still in the ICU. Of course, that didn't stem the flow of his rage. Like clockwork, he did what he had always done, directing his anger at me, calling me terrible names, and saying the most hurtful things. He triggered my long-lived shame.

But by now I had built the strongest of shields and honed the sharpest of swords. We fought like the master and his protégé, defending our respective positions with justifications galore, all the while cutting each other with the harshest of words.

Moments before I was led out of the ICU, his rage increased exponentially, signaling to me that I had cut him deeply. Now safely out of harm's way, I dropped my shield and put away my sword, feeling euphoric that I had won. At that moment, all the shame and fear of being everything he had ever put upon me disappeared. I remember replaying my greatest moment, wielding the final blow and slicing him with the harshest and most hurtful of words, hoping he would feel the same shame and emptiness he had imprisoned me with my entire life. Right then, I felt like a million bucks. I felt free. I felt as if I had finally won.

Several hours later, I received a call from the ICU that he was still enraged and would not relent. The medical staff had strapped him down in an effort to calm him. The charge nurse suggested I come right away. Again, I reluctantly complied, angry that once again he was getting undue attention and being treated like the victim, when really it was me.

It was 4:30 a.m. when I arrived at the hospital. As I entered the ICU, life became surreal. It was eerily quiet. No one was present except my father and me. He was lying on his back, as still as still could be, with restraints still tightly strapped to his arms and legs. I looked into my father's eyes, and for the first time, didn't see anger or contempt, but emptiness, confusion, sadness, and regret.

I don't remember how long I stood there, but I can recall the center of his eyes reflecting directly on mine. I pinched his cheek, somewhat expecting him to awake or do something. But I was in denial. My psyche was not yet ready to accept the reality... that it was Thanksgiving Day and my father was dead...and that I was the catalyst to his rage that ultimately shut off the lights on his life.

My dad, my connection to all I knew about myself, was gone. I stayed numb only for a moment and then began to fight against a feeling of emptiness so deep and powerful it was unlike any I had felt before. It felt like a black hole that ran from the top of my heart to the bottom of my gut.

The intensity of my shame was reminiscent of what it was as a child, when I would hide in the cupboards under the sink, desperate for safety from the rage of my father and the shame of his berating my mother...and my not being able to protect her.

Looking back, I realize that immediately after my father's death I had taken my anger at him and directed it squarely on me, where I was certain it belonged...just as it always had. The euphoria I had experienced over my triumphant win the night before had plunged into my horrific truth— that he was right about me and had always been so. He was the only one who knew the real truth about me; I was everything he had always said I was. And now he was dead and I had a hand in killing him...the only person who really understood me and loved me nonetheless.

I can remember feeling sad and confused in the days and weeks after his death. I reached for alcohol—my long-lost friend—doing everything I could to feel nothing. I was unknowingly taking out tremendous anger and angst, not just on myself, but on those who cared about and tried to support me.

I desperately longed for support and connection, yet ironically, I could not see the obvious, that I was pushing away those who loved and cared for me the most. It was as if I was powerless over a need to suffer.

I remained in a state of shame, guilt, loneliness, and hatred of myself for years. And everyone but me could see that I created it for myself. They did what anyone would do. When I pushed them away, they gave me space. But, from my perspective, I was being taken advantage of, unreasonably criticized, betrayed, singled out, rejected, and ostracized at every turn. I was alone and had done nothing to deserve it.

It wasn't until a few years later that I finally hit rock bottom. With the love and support of several wonderful people, along with weekly therapy (with Mary Earle, to whom I will always be grateful), I managed to climb out of the depths of shame. With help and guidance, I broke the vicious cycle I had fallen into where I relied on anger as a shield to defend myself. Up to then, I had been certain the world saw me the same way I saw myself...and that it was determined to expose me and cause me pain as soon as I let down my guard.

Having not a clue I was doing so, I had memorized a

road of fear and anger destined for self-fulfilling prophecy. For it was my fear of being discovered for the shameful person I believed myself to be that caused me to shield myself from others. I used anger as my sword when they would get too close. So I remained alone and empty, with that black hole inside me constantly reminding me that no one loved me. And I believed no one loved me because my father was always right. I had concluded I wasn't worth loving—the very belief I hoped all my life wasn't true.

A New Perspective

Believe it or not, today I can love my father. I learned to take responsibility for my part in our relationship, to make true amends, and to come to peace with it. I realized that, like me at the time, he couldn't do any better...but I also realized that today, I can. My father had no clue about how his actions affected other people. He was never given the insight that my experience with him gave me. You'd think that it would have been obvious to both of us early on, but to the angry man it never is.

I've worked with hundreds of angry men through the years, and we all lived behind a shield of anger. The anger shield that I see when I look back on my life is unmistakable to me now, but at the time, even though it blocked my view of reality, it was as invisible as the air we breathe. Behind that shield, our perceptions are distorted. We can't see above it or around it. Asking an angry man to change his ways is like asking a blind man to try harder to see. When we can't see beyond our anger, we blame the people closest to us for not changing. We need them to change so that we don't have to and because we don't know how.

The first real step I took toward overcoming my anger and rage was to become honest with myself. This was an incredibly difficult and painful process. My entire life had been built upon a foundation of fear, and as a result, I had focused on keeping my shameful beliefs hidden so as not to be exposed.

Nonetheless, I had to be willing to look at my behavior without justifications, rationalizations, and a host of other mechanisms designed to protect myself from responsibility for my actions.

And I couldn't just think it; I had to feel it, as reliance on thinking had led me to where I was. But I had told myself early on in life that feeling okay about me was the precursor to my experiencing hurt and shame, so thinking would have to be my guide. I had concluded, albeit incorrectly, that it made no sense to rely on instinct and emotion, as they were the causal factors that had gotten me to where I was.

So I used one of the tenets I had learned in a twelve-step program. I wrote out a quasi life story of my anger. I recalled examples and wrote them down, becoming acutely aware of what I had done to others.

It was excruciating at times, as I wrote in such a way that I could not deny the truth. It became starkly obvious that my best efforts to use my thinking as my primary guide in relationships hadn't worked. Those best efforts resulted in my being angry, and subsequently alone, resentful, and distrustful of everyone and everything. The evidence was clear. For there I was, miserable enough to seek out therapy, and completely baffled by my inability to maintain quality relationships with anyone I cared for and vice versa. It became unmistakably clear that it was me—my behavior, and not theirs—that ultimately resulted in my anger and subsequent feelings of shame. It was no longer my father who was the tyrant; for he was gone.

It was me.

But to tell myself was not enough. I was already convinced that I had spent my life wearing a mask and believing myself a fraud. Keeping it to myself would do nothing more than strengthen that belief. So I had to go over my story with someone else. I had to trust...a taboo in my belief system. It would force me to take off my mask, even if just for a few moments, and show what I believed to be the raw, ugly truth about me...and how badly I had hurt others, especially those closest to me.

The thought of acknowledging truths of which I was fully aware felt like emotional suicide. Yet I had hit my bottom and had no one else to blame; nowhere else to put my anger. I remember trying to blame my father, but then acknowledging the obvious—that he couldn't have caused my behavior after years had passed since his death.

These timid first steps were not always onto firm ground. I had to force myself to be open to new ideas. I had to stop fighting to be right all the time. And I had to stop trying to control everyone and everything. Instead, I began to focus on finding a way to be happy.

I became willing, for the first time since I can remember, to try new strategies and new behaviors in every area of my life. And as I persisted, the fear became less and the shield inched down. It was amazing. Everyone and everything began to look different. Without my anger shield protecting me, I was able to see so much more clearly. I began to accept that I wasn't such a bad guy after all. And over time, I began to see more of life without a shield and a sword. I came to accept that the world wasn't as dangerous as I had always believed and that I was not so different from others; that they had internal strife just like me. With each new day, my shield dropped a bit more, allowing me to see even more clearly.

It was like wearing glasses with fuzzy lenses all my life, fighting with everyone that what they saw was wrong and that what I saw was right. And then finding a new pair of glasses, at first not trusting that what I was seeing was real, but, the longer I wore them the more I trusted it was real. And I became able to understand what others were seeing and feeling, and I began to feel connected, accepted, and okay with just being me.

What Life is Like Today

THE author and psychiatrist M. Scott Peck said it best: Life is difficult.

As you just read, I, for better or worse, have been forced to change in order to survive emotionally.

And now, physically.

On July 20, 2010, I was diagnosed with cancer. Melanoma, to be specific. I stayed in denial of the severity of it until after the initial surgery. I was told that the cancer was a "Stage 3B." Having done a bit of research, I knew that the survival rate for someone at my stage was less than twenty percent. My initial feeling may have been fear, but what came out was anger.

I was enraged!

This was no real surprise; we typically resort to our default defenses when cornered or caught off guard. This had been my modus operandi since I was a child. I learned it from my dad. Why stop now, right?

I've been a psychotherapist for over fifteen years, having spent the majority of that time counseling angry men. These are high-performing, hard-working men who thrive in the workplace, but whose lives at home are falling apart. More than half those years I spent as one of them, and the rest evolving into the man I am today.

So while it's true that there was much ugliness in my father, it is also true that he must have suffered tremendously. I never would have thought that before. But I now know it had to be the case because I suffered the same way. Having nothing to compare it to, I just never saw it until I finally changed. Knowing that his sons and closest friends only tolerated, rather than wanted to be with him must have been brutal. It certainly was for me. Little did he know how hard we all tried to hang in there with him. But it was his insistence on pushing us away that made us finally accept that he wasn't going to change and focus more on protecting ourselves. And those who were in my life did the same thing.

For several years now, I have dedicated myself to helping other men who feel and act the way my father and I did. While each has his own unique story, they all tell my story. And I tell theirs. I've become very good at being able to "get inside" the minds of angry men. One reason is because I have felt just like they do. But another reason is that I've become a true mirror of their other side, the one they've always wanted to show but never knew how to bring out.

To tie all this together, my late-stage cancer has compelled me to speak out to a broader audience. While I have no intention of dying, the odds of a shortened life are fairly strong. But I use the "fight" from my dad and the "peace" from my mom not just to stay alive, but to *really live* on a daily basis. Had I not transformed from that angry guy into who I am today, I'd probably be dead by now; or at least well on my way. I saw it happen to my dad—and I had followed his pattern in so many other ways.

So I'm speaking out. I've been given a voice, and I'm using it. I've written this book in hopes that others who have struggled in the isolation and pain of anger can find the help that's available. That they can learn there is a pathway OUT, if they're willing to work at it, and trust people to help them. My track record helping angry guys is remarkable in its success rate. The work is gratifying to me and life-changing for them. Having the knowledge of therapeutic methods and philosophies and the insight that comes from living this story myself, I have an inroad many lack. And it does seem to work. Time and time again, one angry man after another transforms into a caring, loving, and happy man. For guys who haven't trusted anyone and have been in a protective mode most of their lives, the trust they develop as we work together is astonishing and rare.

I want to help angry men and those they love the most. The guy trapped in anger needs to come to terms with the pain, fear, and subsequent shame he experiences, before he can be happy. If I can make a difference in the life of an angry guy, then he can break the cycle of anger that has robbed him, his children, and others who care for and love him. He'll then enjoy true, genuine connections with those he loves and real quality of life. He can then believe in himself and be proud of who he has become. He'll become the man he has always wanted to be.

While I've personally counseled hundreds of angry men, I realize that there are more out there than I could possibly work with. And because I'm committed to helping as many as I can, I've expanded my reach in other ways, including books, publications, professional trainings, and public presentations.

Those in the helping professions need to accurately understand what it's like inside the mind of an angry man in order to be of service. I'm committed to helping those who help guide men like my dad and me. My father dying due to anger...and me, ironically, using the same past to help other angry men (and myself) find themselves and their best—this is what I've got to give. This is what I aspire to share.

I have been forced to change almost everything in my life—physically, emotionally, mentally, and spiritually—and since I will likely depart this world a bit earlier than I had planned, I can't think of a better way to live than to teach and give of myself. The desire alone is luscious.

What a wonderful way to feel alive.

WHY YOU NEED THIS BOOK

A RE you an angry man? Do you know someone who's an angry man? Is he a part of your family? A part of your life?

Too often we try to avoid the topic, and especially the truth, because we're afraid of what it all might mean. Yet the longer you avoid looking at yourself in that proverbial mirror (whether you're the one with the problem or the one trying to control the waves of fury that ride through your home), the longer it will be before you can address it all; the longer it will be before you can take the steps to strengthen the relationships around you; and the longer it will be before you're living the quality of life that you deserve and long for.

And not just you, but all the ones you care about in your life.

Why Only Address the Anger Problem in Men?

In the society we live in, men have permission to be aggressive and self-centered. It's somewhat acceptable and even presumed that anger will be an issue sometimes. Men are still culturally driven and expected to be the breadwinners; the dominant, strong types. Men are supposed to be devoid of emotions, or at least strong enough not to show them. Statistics point to an epidemic of anger in our society, and men overwhelmingly lead the pack.

Women, on the other hand, are expected to express their emotions appropriately, to know how they feel and why. They are (unreasonably) expected to tolerate angry men, relying on their own ability to empathize and maintain relationships. Women are presumed to be better equipped to deal with negative emotions, including anger, in a much more healthy way. Yet this doesn't mean that women don't become angry. They just don't always act it out the same way.

We all have to find that corner of the world where we're most effective. I understand angry men because I was one. I understand their specific pressures, pains, and triggers. I understand how to help. There are others who are effective with women. My corner of the world is angry men.

Eight Simple Questions

The following are eight simple questions designed to help determine whether you or a man you care about has an anger problem.

1. Has it ever been suggested that you might have a problem with anger?
2. Do you sometimes wonder why you get so angry or angry so often?
3. Do you stay angry and bitter at people who have treated you unjustly or unfairly?

4.   Are you impatient or intolerant of yourself and others?

5.   Have you been told (repeatedly) that you have an excessive need to be "right"?

6.   Do you feel, more often than not, that you do not receive the respect that you deserve?

7.   Do you have difficulty letting others get close to you (is it difficult to trust)?

8.   Does it feel like most of your intentions are misinterpreted or misunderstood?

My experience suggests that *if you answered yes to any two questions, you likely have a problem with anger*, or you are right about the person you believe may have such a problem.

The purpose of this book (and the workbook that will follow) is to introduce a structured set of actions and principles that, when applied, will all but extinguish the real causes of unhealthy anger; resulting in a paradigmatic shift in how the angry guy views life and the people in it. This process, if followed precisely, is promised to result in an incredible change of mind and heart.

Deal with the causes...and the symptoms go away. It's simple, but not easy. The process is hard, and sometimes gripping, emotional work. But it's worth a man's committed investment in himself, whatever it takes.

The result? Angry men becoming the quality men they have always wanted to be.

WHO IS THE
ANGRY MAN?

THE angry man is an unhappy man at best. He constantly feels misunderstood. He is often described as abusive—emotionally, verbally, and sometimes physically. He rages like a hurricane, hurting those closest to him the most.

Tragically, the angry man is often unaware that his anger is rooted within him. He just can't understand that external forces are only triggers. He is oblivious that his anger is caused by intense and emotionally painful feelings such as shame, self-hatred, fear of failure, loneliness, and rejection.

His modus operandi is to deflect the storm within, jettisoning it toward someone or something else—usually toward those he loves the most, those less likely to reject him. He is in denial of himself as the real source of his pain. When you spend your life looking out, why would you ever consider looking within?

In moments of fury, the angry man is certain that his aberrant behavior is justified. When most people get angry, they justify their anger but they don't act it out. Let's face it...everyone gets angry. Just think about the last time you were angry about something. Did you feel justified? Did you feel that you had been wronged?

Did you feel sadness or remorse afterward? Angry feelings are normal. In fact, if you don't have moments of anger or frustration, something isn't quite right.

Most people recognize this. If you're nodding along right now, then you understand that in the moment, you don't have the capacity to minimize your anger; you are holding onto it as the result of basic instinct.

The angry man, however, has evolved into a master at skewing perceptions, seeing what is necessary to justify his hurt as the fault of someone or something else, and giving him license to strike out. He is repressing the voice of the heart while feeding that of the mind. For in his heart lives a certainty that he is less valuable than others, a liability in relationships, and destined to a life of struggle. He hopes that somehow he can beat the odds and get away from the misery and loneliness he has always known. Yet, by virtue of his anger, all he does is reinforce it.

For the angry man, being "right" is as close to being happy as he gets. For him, happiness is beyond his reach. He doesn't know what it is, how it feels, or how to attain it. He watches others and tries to emulate the contentment and comfort he sees in them, but the feeling remains elusive. He determines with certainty that he is different, lacking the ability to connect and be "one of the guys."

Thus, he spends his life running from his greatest fear: that he is somehow different in a negative sort of way. His longing and desperation to feel secure and a "part of" something else, something special, results in a life mired in fear, defensiveness, and vigilance—even hyper vigilance. This results in pushing or pulling away from those he wishes to be closest to.

At this moment, you may be thinking to yourself that there's no way this angry man in your life—whether it's you or someone you care about—can be filled with these feelings. The way they act, the things they do, the things they say, all seem to be in direct contrast to what I'm telling you here.

But it's true. The angry man is riddled with fear. That's the crux of the situation. The sooner he realizes and accepts this, the sooner he is able to dig down to the roots of each individual fear and begin to pull out the weeds that lead to anger, leaving a lush garden of hope and happiness in its place.

By his own volition, the angry man tries to be anyone other than himself, unknowingly compensating for his supposed liabilities by acting the opposite of how he genuinely feels. He acts powerful when feeling powerless. He dominates when feeling out of control. He acts with bravado when feeling most insecure. He is critical of others when angry at himself. He works twice as hard when he fears he isn't a good enough employee, friend, or lover, making sure there exists no justification to reject him.

The patterns become clear now, don't they? You're sitting there reading this, maybe rubbing your chin, leaning back in the chair, and thinking, "Oh my, I can definitely see all of this."

But what happens next? Why does all of this good intention, or at least harmless intention, become anger? The reality is that the angry man usually achieves the very scenario he has worked so hard to avoid. His actions consistently result in him feeling better or less than someone else, but never equal, never connected. And when he doesn't obtain the results he wants, things begin to fall apart.

He becomes frustrated, despondent, baffled, and self-conscious. He feels exposed, as if everyone can see how lowly and valueless a person he believes himself to be. And because of this underlying, unaware despondence he feels, our angry man copes as the human species seems to do. He learns how to be who he needs to be to get what he wants (or thinks he needs). He becomes highly attuned to the behaviors of others, tightening and toughening his guard by knowing his foe. Over time, the angry man learns that he can out-manipulate, out-articulate, and prove that he is right even when he knows this isn't the case. He learns to win at any cost. Losing means that the truth he believes about himself will be uncovered. And this, to him, is tantamount to torture.

Every thought, feeling, and action originates from one's fundamental perception of self. Until an angry guy accepts that he holds equal value to the next man, he will not drop his guard. He must accept this truth before real change can take place. Then, and only then, can he see himself, relative to the rest of the world, in a more positive and productive light.

There are a number of things we need to be aware of regarding angry men, if there is to be help or understanding. A few of these things are that:

- Angry men have an inaccurate perception of themselves; albeit unconscious, they always see themselves as "less than" others—never "equal."

Based on his behavior, this is one of the most powerful aspects for those closest to him to understand, and simultaneously accept that only he can decide to acknowledge it.

- Angry men act the opposite of how they really feel, which is powerless and dominated by the world. They attempt to mask this truth through demonstrations of power and control.

- Angry men unknowingly use anger to protect and keep hidden feelings such as shame, sadness, regret, and fear of failure.

- Angry men must accept truths about themselves before they can achieve permanent change. This is a very difficult task. If it was easy, they would have already done it.

- The angry man's internal foundation is infested with shame and self-hatred. He rejects himself. And if he is honest, he will admit feeling alone and feeling neither "connected" to anyone nor a "part of" anything.

- Angry men have learned to "not feel" and to "not trust." They isolate behind an emotional wall of stone. And they lash out hard, usually with the tongue as their sword, to protect and defend against threats that don't even exist.

I'm going to speak clearly and plainly throughout this book. I'm going to be point-blank. Consider this to be a manual, of sorts. My words come from experience as an angry man, but also experience as a therapist who helps those ready for a way out. I don't talk about my issues as an angry man to elevate myself to some higher status; I've merely found it easier for other men dealing with the same issues to connect with me. We can talk from a level footing. I've learned more about myself from my clients than from anyone else. I've learned to listen to my colleagues who have a sincere desire to help me be a better therapist and a better person. I've learned how to help others by my mistakes. And I'll be the first to admit that I make mistakes daily.

One of the important aspects of overcoming your anger is to not expect yourself or others to be perfect. The only people who always fail are those who expect themselves to be perfect. If you maintain a standard of perfection, you're sure to fall far short of that mark. And when your expectations aren't met, it leads to the same result, time and again: anger!

Angry men try to convince others they're special because they fear that they are not. How many times in your life have you been so insecure around other people, so in need of being accepted or liked, that you began to act as though you were more like someone else?

Men often pretend to be different than they are, especially with women. An angry man needs a woman to be impressed by him, as he doesn't see how she could authentically "like" him unless he does something special. He believes that unless he acts in a way that she will find impressive, he will be rejected.

For the angry man, to not feel special or "better" than others is for him to feel "less than." He fears exposure as a liability, assuming that when you find out his lack of worth, you will reject and abandon him without hesitation. He buries his fear behind manufactured illusions that convince him that his frustrations are your fault, and that it is you who should change. That he would not have to get angry if you would just do your part.

If he's willing to put aside his assumptions and certainties and open his mind to a new way of thinking, then he can discover happiness far beyond what he has ever felt. Our angry man:

- Will no longer need validation from others,
- Will find contentment and peace of mind,
- Will discover that resentments will fall by the wayside,
- Won't be so hard on himself or others,
- Will feel trusted and understood,
- Will feel "a part of" versus "outside the circle" in relationships,
- Will be able to ask for help without fear of embarrassment or failure,
- Will be able to trust and let people see the real him,
- Will develop a capacity for healthy, long-term connections in his closest relationships.

While the process is simple, it isn't easy. It requires honesty deeper than most angry men have ever consciously known.

Often, just being honest with ourselves is the biggest challenge to overcome. We look in the mirror, and even when we see the problem staring back at us, we try to rationalize or marginalize it. We are certain that since we can see it, everyone can. So it's difficult to be open. It's easier to hide our true selves.

But we forget that we're our own worst critics. We're the ones who see ourselves through a magnifying glass and focus on all of our own flaws. Believe it or not, other people are actually too busy with their own lives to focus on ours.

This process requires priority and commitment to a new way of conducting our lives and to thinking about the world around us and how we fit into it. The angry man has learned to argue about almost anything. Being right has become the priority over being happy. But approaching this process the way he has approached everything else will get him what he's always gotten, and that's not what anyone wants. He needs to constantly remind himself that there are no shortcuts in this game we call Life. It's one foot in front of the other, one step at a time. Trouble is, angry men love shortcuts, so this concept must be put aside.

If there is any question that trying a new way of life is a good idea, simply ask yourself, "How's my way working for me?" The answer should be obvious. And if you're still reading and curious, then you're open enough to change and have a fighting chance.

THREE TYPES
OF ANGRY MEN

PEOPLE express anger in many different ways. Some highlight their emotions for all to see; they hold no punches, so to speak. Others contain it within and withdraw. Still others lash out in subtle, but just as hurtful ways, without throwing fists or objects or insults. These three types of anger are known as Aggressive, Passive, and Passive-Aggressive.

You've likely heard these terms before, but they might not make sense until you understand them at their core. Let's discuss the three types of anger so that we can all have a firm footing on what we're dealing with. Which one do you see yourself as?

The Aggressive Type

This is the type most people associate with the typical "angry man." He is the man who is hot-tempered, is quick to react to negative stimuli, and lashes out at others. Whether he is throwing his fists, objects, or insults, the intent is to hurt those closest to him.

We tend to read a lot about these aggressive types in the newspapers for arrests, assaults, and other violent behaviors. But that doesn't mean that as long as a person doesn't physically hurt another he is not being aggressive. Emotional harm can be devastating. Calling someone "stupid" or telling her that you hate her can be just as harmful as punching her.

Some of the symptoms of aggressive anger are:

Threats—Trying to make someone cower, whether the threat is of violence, destruction of property, or simply pointing a finger of blame, is an example of aggressive behavior. So are the clothes you wear and the way you drive. If you wear a shirt with a picture of a gun facing someone else, that's aggressive. If you tailgate, or honk your horn at other cars, you're being threatening.

Hurtfulness—Physically assaulting someone, destroying property, making crude jokes, lying, and breaking the trust of a friend are all acts of hurtfulness. Swearing can also be hurtful to another, though in today's environment, it has become somewhat normalized. Also, labeling or categorizing others can be hurtful behavior. If you see a gay couple and know nothing about them, but you call them a derogatory name as they walk by, specifically because they're gay, you're being hurtful.

Destructiveness—Abusing drugs or alcohol is considered destructive behavior focused on yourself (didn't realize that, did you?). When you drive recklessly, you're driving aggressively, putting others at risk due to insensitive behavior. Breaking things and treating animals poorly are also examples of destructive behavior.

Bullying—Bullying is gaining a great deal of attention lately. When you target a weaker person and bully them, you're doing so to try and hide an insecurity within you. This behavior can be quite aggressive and injurious to the other party.

Extreme Behavior—Extreme behavior can sometimes be considered aggressive. Driving too fast, speaking very quickly, and even spending money compulsively can be deemed aggressive. Extreme behaviors are usually symptomatic of attempts to cover for some internal conflict.

Grandiosity—Look no further than professional sports and you'll see some athletes (not all) who rationalize that they deserve more respect than others because of their talent and performance on the field. The vast majority of angry men I work with are high performance type guys and see themselves in a similar light. They justify their "I deserve better than you" attitude, and expect those closest to them to appreciate their accomplishments, understand their unique pressures, and then give them a pass when they hurt others. Yet at the same time, they live in fear that if they are not successful, they will receive no respect or appreciation at all. They treat themselves conditionally; and then do the same to those closest to them and those they love the most.

I tell them, "You can't give what you don't have and you will give what you do have." And let's face it; society reinforces conditional behavior, so it makes it even more difficult to convince the angry man give up his "I'm special" ideology.

Selfishness—If one ignores others' needs, whether physical or emotional, then he needs to ask himself why. This is self-centered, "it's all about me," behavior. If he doesn't see the benefit to him, then it's not important. Selfishness is seen as very aggressive by the recipient.

Vengeance—We've all wanted to pay back someone else for wrongs or implied wrongs done to us, but holding on to that desire for vengeance fuels aggressive thinking, feeling, and behavior.

Vengeance and resentment are always about the past. Angry men will hang on to vengeance and resentment for what seems like forever, even after the event has passed and everyone but them has moved on.

The Passive Type

The Passive type acts out his anger completely different from the aggressive type, but he is just as angry. He usually withdraws and turns his anger inward. This type of angry man tends to appear depressed and critical of himself quite often. He justifies being lonely and alone as proof that he's not worthy of another's company, or that he's powerless over the fact that nobody likes him.

A peculiar aspect of the passive type is that they tend to punish themselves to get back at others, rationalizing that their misery will make the person they hold responsible feel guilty. They are covert, diligently keeping score, and constantly adding up all the times they've been wronged. They retaliate via passive control—becoming helpless, needy, and high maintenance. Through passive behavior, they say to those they feel have wronged them, "You made me angry so now I'll make you feel guilty for it. Now you will have to pay the price. Now you will have to focus on me and my needs."

A risk of being prone to passive-type anger is that one can withdraw to the extent that extreme depression and thoughts of suicide, or even homicide, may become quite real.

If you've ever been in an argument with a passive type angry man, then you've noticed that when he is confronted directly, he becomes silent and walks away. For relationships, this can be devastating. He's angry and trying to punish and control you with his silence, believing that you will eventually give up the conflict and let him have his way. And even though he may win the battle, he ultimately loses the war, as issues never get resolved. Thus, he continues to withdraw even more—often resulting in the loss of the very relationship he was fighting for.

Some of the symptoms of passive anger are:

Secretive Behaviors—When an angry man keeps things to himself, makes comments under his breath, avoids eye contact, or tends to keep his whereabouts vague, he's demonstrating secretive passive-type anger. When he's secretive, he feels in control, for he knows something or has information that you don't. Isolating, stealing, and filing anonymous complaints at work are examples of secretive behaviors.

Psychological Manipulation—When an angry man covertly incites conflict between two other people, he is triangulating; a manipulative tactic designed to get his anger out vicariously through a conflict he creates between others. Not expressing himself when obviously upset, consistently being late, faking illnesses, and manipulating others into feeling guilty for not taking care of his needs are all examples of psychological manipulation.

Self-Blame—At some point, most of us have blamed ourselves for one thing or another. But the passive-type angry man apologizes far too often, is overly self-critical and rejects opportunities for fun or the friendship of others. He will help others but not take care of himself, subsequently not meeting his own responsibilities. Faced with conflict he might say, "What did I do wrong this time?" rather than address the conflict assertively. These are all examples of self-blame.

Ineffectualness—Where there is a pervasive pattern of self-defeating behavior, there is passive-type anger. Being accident-prone, consistently needy, quitting projects, and not being responsible are examples of passive ways to be ineffective.

Dispassion—Overeating, oversleeping, and acting as if he just doesn't care about himself are examples of dispassion. For example, if a passive-type angry man felt treated unfairly, he would likely show no emotion, and instead, internalize the anger and displace that negative energy on something or someone else—likely himself.

Obsessive Compulsive Behavior—Ah, the famous obsessive-compulsive behavior. Constantly checking things, being concerned with extreme neatness, and having set rituals can all be signs of the passive-type trying to suppress his anger. When his ritual is made difficult for him, the passive-type angry man will stew, obsess, and become resentful; eventually looking to even the score, which he usually does through covert behavior.

The Passive-Aggressive Type

Passive-Aggressive anger is perhaps the most insidious of the three types of anger. The passive-aggressive man is only overt when covert means do not achieve his goal. He carries what I like to call "silent rage."

An example of passive-aggressive behavior might look like this: A man responds to his wife, who just purchased a new outfit for a wedding celebration. She asks her husband, "How do I look?" He responds with sincerity, "Great honey...you look great!" And for a moment she is thrilled, enjoying the validation. But a few moments later, for no apparent reason he adds, "That is, if you're going to a rodeo," expressing no emotion or rationale for this comment. While he would never admit that the latter statement was intended to hurt her, clearly it was. But in truth, his comment could be taken either seriously or as a joke. Thus, should she express hurt feelings, he is in a position to make her the poor sport and feel even worse.

The passive-aggressive man described above is angry. It might be that his wife had decided to attend the wedding when he had decided not to go. Or maybe he was envious that she was so excited to attend without him. Regardless of what his thinking was, he decided that she was responsible for his anger. So rather than say so and be vulnerable to feeling "less than," he decided to punish her covertly, hurting her feelings and justifying his actions by doing to her what he had unjustly decided she has done to him. In other words, he doesn't get mad... he gets even.

Some of the symptoms of passive-aggressive behavior are:

Intentional Language—The words we choose can have a lasting impact on others. The passive-aggressive type will often become less emotional the more escalated a conflict becomes. He might be sarcastic, vague, or belittling. He might make excuses that seem reasonable on the surface but are really intended to deflect the matter at hand. He might be ambiguous or circular in his arguments, almost laughing at your feelings. He likely says hurtful things or says things in a hurtful way, and then blames you for reacting with anger and emotion. The passive-aggressive man will say (or not say) whatever is needed for him to get his way.

Sulking—The passive-aggressive type angry man is unwilling to risk being vulnerable. Therefore, he cannot afford to be assertive. So in order to communicate anger or displeasure, he sulks, stomps, sighs loudly, becomes nonresponsive, or a combination of the above, all in an attempt to get the attention he wants when he wants it, without having to express how he genuinely feels. He makes everyone around him uncomfortable until his wants are satisfied.

Avoids Saying No—The passive-aggressive man cannot afford to say "no," as this leaves him open to conflict and rejection. So he is ambiguous, vague, or indecisive. "Ask me later" or "Maybe" are common responses the passive-aggressive man will use to skirt around having to say "No."

Overcritical—Some passive-aggressive men will point out everything they believe is wrong with you. They do this in an attempt to gain or maintain a sense of control, meticulously criticizing those around them, especially those closest to them and those with authority. And when confronted with his behavior, the angry man might say, "Well, it's true, isn't it? I'm just trying to help you be the best you can be. Is there something wrong with that?" And then he proceeds to criticize further for your being "too sensitive."

In order to not take the angry man's behavior any more personal than necessary, it's important to understand which anger type he emulates the most.

And if you are an angry man, one or more of the classifications listed above will have felt like you were staring into a mirror. Willingness to keep reading and courage to acknowledge the truth are now necessities, as you are about to swallow some big chunks of truth about yourself.

THE ANGER CYCLE

If you've ever spent time with an angry man, you know how it feels to be on the receiving end of inappropriate anger. What I describe as "The Anger Cycle" will help you understand this unconscious process and why he repeatedly does what he does.

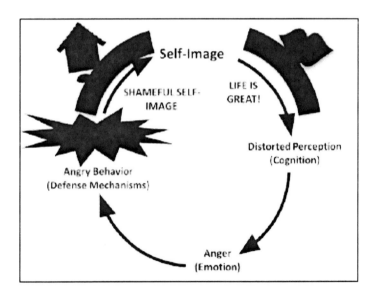

Self-Image

SHAMEFUL SELF-IMAGE

LIFE IS GREAT!

Distorted Perception (Cognition)

Angry Behavior (Defense Mechanisms)

Anger (Emotion)

The crux of the Anger Cycle suggests that the point where the angry man blows up or shuts down (the flash point) may be a goal, but unconsciously *it is not his ultimate goal.* Years of self-examination and clinical observation of other angry men suggest that his acting out behavior is only a vehicle to help him reach his ultimate goal—*an intense feeling of shame.*

That's right. Shame.

Shame is the core of the angry man's self-image. The flash point, where he acts out his anger, eventually leaves him feeling "less than" and ashamed—the very feelings he's been running from all his life.

We all unconsciously strive for that which we believe we deserve. The angry man has never felt deserving, for he genuinely believes, albeit unconsciously, that he is less than everyone else "just because." His self-image is the core component that determines his belief of who he is relative to the rest of the world. His self-image must change in order for there to be a paradigm shift in feelings, thoughts, and behaviors.

Self-Image

The creation of the self-image is believed by some to be rooted in genetics. Others suggest it to originate from our experiences and environment. Wherever that true beginning is, it becomes the foundation of a self-image that will determine our perception of who we are and what we deserve throughout our lives.

Everything else we think, feel, and do will be built upon this perception of self.

The Angry Man tends to trudge through life with a self-image that tells him he is inadequate and "less than." Subsequently, the world and everyone in it, is, by default, a threat.

And this explains why the angry man is often described as defensive. He doesn't awake consciously feeling different from the next man. Instead, his underlying, unconscious shameful self-image defines his conscious perception of self relative to other people, places, and things. His core perception of self has been the same since he first discovered his self-image.

If someone tells you that the wall is purple when you've been led all your life to believe that it's white, you're not going to believe that it's purple.

In the same way, if my life-long perception of me is based on a self-image that says "I'm inadequate," then even though I see everybody else as adequate, my perception of me will be distorted—that I am different from everybody else "just because." And since this distorted view is unconscious, my conscious thinking about how I will approach a world in which I am inadequate and ill-equipped will be severely skewed as well, as will the behaviors that follow.

It basically comes down to this: I see myself relative to the rest of the world and determine, based on an underlying low self-image, that everyone else is more powerful, more capable, better liked, and more deserving of good relationships than I; all for reasons I cannot explain.

As the result of this powerful underlying self-image, my unconscious centers on my need to protect and defend from being exposed for the fraud I believe that I have to be in order to get by in the world.

But then, a person, place, or situation triggers my distorted perception of self (that I'm "less than"), which triggers a need to protect being exposed as such, which triggers defensive thoughts, which triggers fear, which triggers anger and angry behavior. Suddenly, I become—and remain—reactive and over vigilant. I act out and people respond accordingly, rejecting my behavior, which I perceive as rejecting "me," and I experience the very feelings that I've been running from and trying to hide all my life—pain, fear, and shame. I have succeeded, again, in creating a self-fulfilling prophecy—unconsciously confirming a self-image that has always insisted that I am damaged goods "just because."

Throughout the angry man's life, he repeatedly makes decisions and takes actions to prove to himself that his perceptions and assumptions are correct, that he really is less than (i.e., that the wall really is purple). He is constantly setting himself up to fail. Maybe he'll over generalize or create crisis due to fear of failure, or maybe he'll leap to a conclusion with no basis. For example, he might say, "My car stopped running. Great, now I'm going to have to get a new car," when in reality, he has no idea what is wrong with the car. It might just need a quick adjustment.

Angry men unconsciously find reasons to feel frightened and victimized, especially by those closest to them. It has been my experience and observation that his fear will always be proportionate with what his self-image says he deserves.

If the car breaking down were to trigger the Anger Cycle in me, here's an example of how it might play out:

The car stalls. I immediately determine (incorrectly, based on the distorted perception that I should be perfect and nothing should ever go wrong or that I must have been irresponsible for being unprepared) that the car stalling was my fault, which triggers anger in the form of severe criticism of myself, which results in feelings of powerlessness and inadequacy, which is exactly what I have tried to keep from happening.

Next, I feel afraid, because I'm sure others can now see me the same way I see myself—powerless and inadequate. As a result, my fear of being exposed becomes intense. I become hyper-critical of myself for being what I perceive as "less than." But rather than own my irrational behavior, I blame it on the car, the mechanic, and all the people driving past me—not stopping to help or giving a hoot about me.

I again focus on the worst possible scenario—that I'm going to have to buy a new car—but now I make the problem worse by focusing on the fact that I don't have the money (which is, of course, also my fault and more proof that I'm a loser).

Finally, I conclude, with absolute certainty, that I'll lose my job because I don't have a car, which will result in the loss of my house, which will result in the loss of my girlfriend and friends, as they'll finally see me for the loser I really am. Note: This entire scenario plays out in my head and heart within seconds.

Suddenly, the world that I've worked so hard to control and manipulate, that I've paraded around as superior to yours, begins to crumble. It's no wonder I blow up. I see all my control and ability to manipulate as slipping away. My thoughts are to defend against losing everything I value. I feel powerless, vulnerable, and alone...just like

I felt as a kid.

This is the unconscious course of the Anger Cycle. But understanding it and dealing with it are two completely different things, so let's discuss the other basic tenants that make up the Anger Cycle.

Distorted Perceptions

When our thinking becomes distorted, we over generalize or overestimate how hard it's going to be to deal with something or someone (because we are already concerned about losing or failing), or we develop conclusions based on a minimal amount of information (such as in the previous example with the car). Ultimately, we find a way or reason to feel frightened and victimized by the rest of the world.

An angry man's distorted perceptions will always result in negative consequences...always.

Distorted perceptions seem logical and rational but they're not, even though we're certain of them at the moment. Distorted perceptions reflect the angry man's low self-image. They feed his fear and subsequent defensive behaviors. They make healthy resolution unattainable.

Below are some of the ways he thinks that leads to distorted perceptions:

All-Or-Nothing—He sees things as black or white; there's no gray area. It's win or lose, right or wrong.

Overgeneralization—When something goes wrong—it could be anything—the angry man will see it as a neverending pattern of defeat.

Mental Filter—He chooses one negative event and focuses on it to the exclusion of all others. I tell the men I work with, "What you focus on will always get bigger."

Disqualifying the Positive—He dismisses positive experiences and says "they don't count," rarely giving himself credit, except when he needs to feel superior to you.

Jumping to Conclusions—Even when there are no negative facts present, he works himself up by assuming the worst.

Mind Reading—He is certain that he knows what others are thinking and feeling and reacts based on these beliefs.

Fortune-Teller—He assumes that things are going to turn out the way he thinks they will, and he reacts based purely on assumptions.

Magnification and Minimization—He tends to exaggerate things, whether making them larger or smaller than they really are; minimizing his part in mistakes and maximizing his part in successes.

Emotional Reasoning—He feels a certain way, so it must be true, right? This is often not the case, but this distortion helps him justify irrational feelings.

Should Statements—He relies on the words "should" and "shouldn't." When should or shouldn't statements are directed towards you, he is focused on you so that he doesn't have to look at himself.

Labeling—When he makes a mistake, he labels himself a "loser." This is a common distortion among angry men. They determine their worth based solely on behavior. He doesn't recognize his intrinsic value. It's all about performance.

Being able to identify our distorted perceptions is necessary to gain a more accurate awareness of reality. All of us experience distorted perceptions, but angry men are notorious for interpreting relationships from a highly distorted perspective, completely oblivious to the possibility that they might be wrong. Their distorted perceptions don't allow them to acknowledge that their beliefs about themselves and the world might all be a mistake.

Defense Mechanisms

We use defense mechanisms to protect ourselves from harm or from perceived harm. Angry men also use defense mechanisms to conveniently and effectively rearrange priorities and responsibilities, which helps them to avoid dealing with reality.

Two of these defense mechanisms are Denial and Distortion. It's important to note that there are many other defense mechanisms we all rely upon at different times. But Denial and Distortion are commonly utilized by angry men. We'll get into the other mechanisms shortly.

Common Defenses Among Angry Men

Denial—He refuses to accept life and his circumstances as they are. When circumstances are either to threatening or too risky, he will partially or entirely deny their existence. Angry men remain in denial of their problems due to fear that addressing them will result in the need to give up protection of their emotional pain and shame.

Distortion—This occurs when a person reshapes the reality around him to meet what he needs most from within. For example, he might manipulate you to get the validation he wants, when in reality he needs to get it from himself.

Common Defenses Among Adults

The following defense mechanisms are common among all of us and are considered moderate to mild in nature. While these defense mechanisms may offer us short-term benefits, they can also create lasting problems in relationships, work, and our overall enjoyment of life.

Displacement—When you're angry with your spouse but take that anger out on your children, you're displacing your emotions.

Dissociation—Putting off dealing with emotions, usually during duress. We tend to do this when our psyche can't handle the powerful emotions evoked in the moment. For example, a person who can recount a brutal crime with no change in emotion might be dissociating.

Isolation—Being emotionally detached. It is not necessary to be physically isolated in order to experience the same emotionally. One could be in a crowd of fifty people and still feel alone. This would be an example of emotional isolation.

Intellectualization—Using the intellectual aspects of a given situation in order to detach or disconnect from the accompanying emotion. "If my boss had listened to the whole situation he wouldn't have fired me," could be an example of an angry man who was fired for constant arguing but is choosing to focus on irrelevant details so as to avoid dealing with feelings accompanying the real reason for his being fired.

Reaction Formation—Converting unmanageable emotions and situations into manageable ones. This is the process of our psyche altering reality (distorting perceptions) to help it avoid dealing with feelings or situations too big for our insides to handle directly. For example, I had a client whose father would make him watch as the father beat his mother every night. When I asked about it, he smiled and laughed. I asked what he found funny about it and he said, "Nothing. It's not funny at all and I don't know why I'm laughing. I just can't help it." He laughed uncontrollably for several minutes. His psyche was creating the opposite reaction so as to protect him from feelings too big to handle.

Suppression—Consciously minimizing feelings to the point that they are no longer taxing with the hope that the feeling and associated thought will eventually be forgotten and not have to be dealt with. The angry man spends a lifetime unaware that he is pushing feelings from his childhood away. This is one reason he relies so heavily on logic and thinking, minimizing how he feels.

Regression—When faced with difficulties or challenges, he reverts to an earlier stage of development which helps him avoid dealing with adult issues in an adult manner. A mild form of regression might be having a temper tantrum.

Rationalization—When you try to convince yourself that something has (or hasn't) happened when in fact, it hasn't (or has).

The following defense mechanisms are common among adults, and are considered healthy for the most part, though they come from a more immature stage of development. These defense mechanisms help us to maintain a degree of control, and relieve us of having to cope with extreme fear and anxiety.

Anticipation—Expecting an event or scenario to go wrong, even when there's no basis for the expectation. This allows us to not be caught off guard.

Humor—Using humor is a powerful way for people to deflect attention from people, places, and things that cause them anxiety and concern. Laughter therapy is considered a legitimate way to deal with problems and improve both mental and physical health.

Identification—Modeling too many behaviors or actions after someone else. It's a great way not to deal with you. Kids will do this with sports heroes. But for adults to do the same would be considered aberrant behavior.

Sublimation—Experiencing negative feelings but turning them into positive feelings, actions, and behaviors. For example, when I was first diagnosed with cancer, I threw myself into my work, determined to stay so busy I couldn't think about my illness. A close friend sat me down and forced me to feel the reality of what was happening. I was sublimating by working so much that I didn't have the time to feel.

Repression—Similar to suppression but more powerful. It is the unconscious avoidance of emotions or circumstances anchored in reality. It is a way to deny that which could cause extreme anxiety or distress. For example, some men and women who have suffered sexual abuse as children have memories and feelings that are repressed.

The following defense mechanisms are more common among adolescents, but they can carry through to adulthood.

Fantasy—To constantly imagine circumstances different than your reality helps avoid day to day problems. For example, a 16 year old having difficulty with classes might feel anxious and critical of himself, but he becomes preoccupied with a new idea. He says, "I don't need school...I'm going to play professional sports."

Projection—Attributing feelings about ourselves onto others. During the writing of this book I've been eating too much sugar. My daughter came home yesterday and scooped herself some ice cream. I became immediately concerned that ice cream would mess with her sugar levels. So I gave her a lecture on nutrition. I was projecting on her my feelings and concerns about *my* eating habits.

Acting Out—When we can't or don't want to deal with painful feelings, and we don't want to talk about them, we tend to act out inappropriately. This may help us feel better temporarily but is usually at another's expense. I tell my clients, "You can talk it out or act it out, but it's going to come out."

THE ANGER SHIELD

The Anger Shield is the result of a need for emotional protection. That "need" for protection might be inaccurate—it might be due to a distorted perception—but regardless of its origin, it's rooted in the desire to protect oneself.

The Anger Shield might be thought of as an umbrella that one throws up over his head to protect against the acid rain falling from the sky. It's the winter coat, hat, and gloves put on to protect against the cold. It's the emotional disconnect that a person develops after being hurt in a previous relationship. The Anger Shield helps protect from getting hurt again.

Just as a warrior would put up a shield to protect himself from the enemy, angry men put up shields to protect themselves from perceived threats of emotional harm.

For example, if I perceive that someone is going to hurt my feelings, shame me, ridicule me, or belittle me—anything that will make me feel bad or scared—I'll throw up the Anger Shield. And that seems to be our nature—what we as angry men tend to do. It's a learned behavior that feels like an instinctive reaction to emotional harm.

Here's an example that I consistently talk through with a client: I ask him to imagine driving behind a truck or a dump truck, when suddenly a rock flies off the truck and it's coming right at him. It's coming so fast that he doesn't have time to protect himself. I ask him, "What would be the first thing you would do?" He'll generally sit and think about it, trying to figure out what he's supposed to say. But the question is simple: What are you going to do? He might say that he's going to move out of the way. And I'll tell him, "No, you're not going to just move out of the way. You won't have time."

I'll ask him again. But by this time he's baffled, just trying to figure out what I'm getting at, but he can't because he's never considered this idea. I tell him, "What you're going to do is protect yourself with your arms!" And he says, "Oh yeah..." It's an instinctive reaction; we put our arms up to protect ourselves.

But then I'll ask him another question. I ask, "Why is it okay to get hit in the arms but not in the face? After all, they're both parts of the body, right?" And he gets it, that ultimately it comes down to a question of damage control. Isn't it better to get a broken arm than a broken face? Sure it is.

We protect ourselves the same way emotionally. When someone is attempting to belittle us, or at least we perceive that to be what's going on, our anger shield goes up in defense to either keep them out and protect ourselves on the inside or to just extinguish the threat...anything other than forcing us to experience that sense of embarrassment and belittlement. The angry man would rather have them deal with his shield, his anger, or his defenses. It makes more sense to him than having to endure the pain and harm that shame and embarrassment can cause.

It's all about vulnerability. Consider my definition for shame:

If everyone else is at a middle point, then I'm two steps lower "just because." I have no rationale to explain why I feel this way, but I'm certain that I'm less of a human being than you and everyone else. I know it, I feel it, and I can give you a million reasons why, even though I know that none of the reasons make sense.

That's how the angry mind works and perceives. But it's learned behavior. That's key. Because if it can be learned, it can be unlearned.

The Anger Shield is one of the first concepts I explain to my clients. It was born out of necessity, as it's one of the first questions I get. Almost every guy I've worked will, at one time or another, say "I don't even know why I get angry."

Sound familiar? Of course it does. We can go for days on end trying to figure out why we are angry and still not come up with a legitimate reason.

Let me give you an example of an experience I had with a past client. The conversation went something like this:

Client: "Yeah, I guess I do have a lot of anger. I don't even know why I do it (yell). I don't want my kids to feel about me how I felt about my dad, and I can see it already." Then a long pause....

I don't move a muscle. I've heard it a hundred times before. I can see myself in his spot, not wanting to repeat the anger of my father but knowing I am nonetheless... and still feeling helpless to stop it.

Then the client says, "All right, so I admit it. I guess

I might have a little anger problem. So now what? How am I supposed to fix it?"

I ask him, "If you don't know why you get angry, then you really don't know what to fix, right? I mean, if you're a mechanic and you can't figure out why the car isn't starting, then you can't fix it until you do, right?"

Client: "I can see that."

What I've learned about myself and the men I've worked with is this: the degree of anger we express is directly proportionate to the degree of fear that we're experiencing.

Let that sink in for a moment. The level of anger you display is directly proportional to the fear that you feel.

Wow. Really? Yes, really.

So, first and foremost, we have to get hardcore honest with ourselves and acknowledge that we are angry men. Only then can we see the shield that we constantly raise, and only then can we recognize the instinctual protective maneuvers that we make with our words, as well as our actions.

Once again: the shield is a metaphor. Just as we throw our arms up to protect our face, we throw our anger out to protect our pain and shame. The shield may be raised a bit differently from one person to the next, but really our shields are all the same. When we start to recognize the instinct to raise our shield, we can start to work on identifying the pain that we are trying to protect and ultimately become aware of the fear that drives our shields to rise. Only then will we be able to put the shield down. And where there is no shield, there is no sword.

And this is good.

When you're standing on the other side of a sliding glass door and someone suddenly sprays the hose at you, you flinch. With enough time, patience, and practice, you will learn not to flinch. And this is what the angry man needs. He needs to learn not to grab his shield as his first option, especially when the result is hurting those he loves the most.

THE 5 "A"S OF ANGER

OVERCOMING anger is a process. It's not going to happen overnight. And you don't have to go it alone. I'm writing this book to guide you through the process and walk you along this path that winds and bends, twists and turns, climbs and dips.

The purpose of this book is to help you understand the basis of your anger, why you feel and do the things that you do, and how to move past it all. If you are sincerely willing, I can help you help yourself change that which causes you and those you love so much pain.

Men who come to see me want to do with their anger what they try to do with everyone and everything else in life: fix it. After being torn down and tacitly admitting a problem, they ask the big question, "So how do I fix it?"

This is a simple way to ask a very complex question. I could write a thousand pages and still not be accurate, as the work we do is cathartic. It's based on process and not skill or technique. It's a metamorphosis...a true transformation of perception and fundamental ideas.

The solution manifests through "what we do" versus "what we say." It's fluid rather than static. There is a definite beginning but no real end.

One might compare the process to that of a car going through a car wash. If the process works, the car enters dirty and comes out clean. But are we able to tell when it actually becomes clean? Do we definitively know which step in the process—the brushing, rinsing, or soaping— is responsible for actually "cleaning" the car? No, but if successful, we know that the car has changed appearance. It's no longer dirty. It has changed.

The above example explains the actual answer to the question "How do I fix it?" I use a generalized a summary of the steps below to give my clients a rough idea of "what we are going to do."

Remember that each of us is a bit different. Therefore, there is no set program, yet the process is always the same. The steps ebb and flow, backward and forward, but the process remains constant, and it continues throughout our lives. For the angry guy, this is the map to positive change and growth. This is the process he must undertake and continue for him to become, and remain, the quality man he has always wanted to be.

The 5 "A"s of ANGER

ACTION:

First and foremost, no matter how hard or how long it takes, the angry guy must be willing to take action. If not, nothing will change. He can be resistant, throw a tantrum, and spit fire—but as long as he does the minimum he will change.

Contrary to what he says, *thinking* his way into positive action isn't going to happen. He's proven this to himself and others time and time again. Eventually, he must commit to this process as a doctrine under which he will live his life. For me, this is fact. Until I was willing to take the necessary steps, I could not find permanent, positive change...period. In addition, he must be willing to follow directions. He doesn't like that idea. He believes it to be like wearing a T-shirt with big bold letters that say, "I Don't Know Anything," and "I don't know." But regardless of how he feels, he must follow directions to get from where he is to where he wants to be.

And finally, he must know his own story, just like I know mine. If he doesn't know or can't admit where he's come from (emotionally), then he can't possibly know where he wants to go.

So he pulls out paper and pencil (not the computer!) and starts writing. He writes what I call an "angerography," a quasi autobiography about his anger and how it has affected his life and those closest to him.

Remembering his previous commitment to action and following directions, he needs to try hard not to think too much. He needs to just do what I suggest whether he believes it to be important or not. I have yet to work with a man who's regretted this process or said that it was a waste of time.

AWARENESS:

If our angry man is honest in writing his angerography, he will begin to experience feelings he has suppressed all the years since he was a child. His feelings will feel as intense and real as if they had occurred just yesterday. He will begin to develop awareness of how he genuinely feels. This is when he starts to emotionally thaw.

He will begin to remember and feel the hurt, fear, and feelings of shame. Whether his perceptions were right or wrong, then or now, makes no difference. They were what they were and are what they are. And those feelings are determining (and have historically determined) his perception of himself relative to the rest of the world. Nothing makes an angry guy cringe more than committing to the expression of feelings; especially those he thought he had escaped so long ago. Whether he realizes it or not, he's spent his life running—acting out through anger much of what he didn't feel safe enough to discuss.

Awareness hurts. It isn't always fun. That's why he went out of his way to forget and minimize those painful childhood experiences. But it's important for him to feel what he experienced back then and not continue the façade of what he has made the past out to be.

So he again takes paper and pencil in hand and draws a line down the middle of the paper. He reviews his story line by line, listing specific incidents in the column on the right. He identifies corresponding feelings that he has protected behind his anger shield and lists them on the left. If two or more of the same feelings are identified but in different places, he writes them down as separate, as the circumstances may have been different.

Again, he must follow these directions exactly, as he will be tempted to hedge a bit regarding his most difficult feelings. But he needs to stay the course. In the end, he will be glad he did.

ACKNOWLEDGMENT:

While awareness is fueled by emotion, acknowledgement is fueled by cognition (thinking). It becomes hard for our angry man to deny that as a little boy he felt confused, scared, and less than all the other kids; maybe just plain powerless. If he is honest with himself, examples from his angerography will surely convince him that things were not quite right and that he was affected in ways he had not felt, thought about, nor talked about for a long, long time...if ever.

He comes to understand how his perceptions of the world got to where they are, and might not be as accurate as he had always believed them to be.

ACCEPTANCE:

It's one thing to acknowledge the truth. It's another thing to accept it. Consider yourself in the following scenario. You are at the circus, amazed at the performers on the high wire. You watch in wonder as one wirewalker climbs onto a fellow performer's shoulders. You hold your breath as they walk across the wire. What do you feel? Maybe some anxiety that they might fall? Amazement that they don't? Whatever the case, you probably find it entertaining, and you probably don't feel flooded with feelings of terror that the circus performers might fall.

Now imagine there to be a break in the action. The circus master pulls you from the crowd and asks, "Do you like the high wire act?," and you reply, "It's great!" He asks, "Are you worried that they might fall?" and you reply, "Just a little, but I doubt they would be up there if they didn't know what they were doing." The circus master then replies, "Good! Because now we would like you to climb the ladder and onto the shoulders of the high wire performer!"

What do you feel now? Do you feel the same as you did when just watching? I think not. Thus, acknowledgment is a cognitive process. Acceptance is an emotional one. The former is made up of thoughts based on belief while the latter is made up of feelings based on actions.

AMENDS:
Apologies are words. Amends are actions.

This is when we step up and try to understand rather than be understood. We've hammered those closest to us with anger. We cannot expect to really know what they are feeling unless we are willing to draw from the feelings we have acknowledged and accepted in previous steps.

Rather than focusing on our need to be heard, we need to focus on their need for us to listen. We need to listen for how we made them feel. We need to leave our self-centeredness behind and make them the priority—no exceptions. We must draw upon our childhood experiences of fear, hurt, and shame in order to connect with the hurt and pain we have caused them. It doesn't matter that we already know or don't want to know that we've caused a loved one a tremendous amount of hurt.

We try to create an environment where they feel comfortable talking and then we need to let them talk. If we don't do this, we will eventually find ourselves back at step one.

Making sincere amends is the key to finding internal peace. How others react to your amends is out of your control. Your job is to clean your side of the street, cease the hurtful behavior, and continue to grow—that's it. There is nothing more you can do.

The 5 "A"s of Anger is a general overview of the process of change. If you follow these steps unconditionally, you will change. I guarantee it.

HOW TO CONTEND
WITH AN ANGRY MAN

Below are strategies to protect one's feelings when faced with the wrath of an angry man:

- *Develop and maintain personal boundaries.*
  You are responsible for the way you are treated. Expecting him to change and treat you the way you deserve to be treated is wishful thinking.

- *Identify the angry man's dominant style.*
  Earlier in this book, I describe specific characteristics of the three different types of angry men. Go back and ask yourself which of the three types best describes the man you are dealing with. He's no doubt a little of each, but he will fit one type better than the other two.

- *Identify their primary defense mechanisms.*
  I also describe the most common defense mechanisms angry men rely on to shield themselves from those who get too close. Learn them and you'll feel much more in control of your own emotions. And it will be easier to maintain a healthy boundary.

- *Address their feelings and not their words.*
  Trying to talk to his issues is like talking to a wall. You are focused on resolve while his focus is on protection. Speak to what he feels and he will deescalate.
  Remember that his fear undermines his feelings. Even though he lives his life in a protective mode, what he really wants is to connect. He just doesn't know how and unconsciously he doesn't believe he deserves to get it.

- *Develop an outside network of support.*
  Angry men assault others with their tongues and their lungs. So be sure you have a network of support. Even if you falter at every turn, having that support network can nullify the pain he instills in you before it gets too deep.

- *Practice positive and repetitive self-talk.*
  Internal, repetitive messages are powerful. I use positive self-talk to fight my cancer. I teach the men I work with to change fear-based messages to positive and empowering ones. Stick positive affirmations on your refrigerator, the dashboard of your car, and anywhere else you'll see them. Carry an item in your pocket to remind yourself of your responsibility to affirm your worth. Tell yourself what you would tell a best friend.

- *Don't fight to be right.*
  Fighting to be right is nothing more than getting

caught up in a power struggle. Ask yourself: Do I want to be right or do I want to be happy? Sometimes we have to pick one. Besides, he will never relent. He has to win. So he will fight to the end.

- *Respond rather than react.*
  We react when we feel powerless and respond when we feel empowered. Stay calm and take care of your feelings. Don't worry about his.

- *Deal with only one issue at a time.*
  Stay focused and refuse to talk about anything other than the matter at hand. His frustration is not your problem unless you let it be.

- *Always maintain a clear path to an exit.*
  Physical safety is number one, but emotional abuse is a good reason to get away as well. When he gets angry, maintain a clear path to an exit. This way, you always have the option to walk away, which is sometimes what you need to do to take care of yourself.

COMMON QUESTIONS
ABOUT ANGRY MEN

Why does my husband act like an angel outside our house but is completely the opposite at home?

IRONICALLY, the angry man will act the worst with those he loves the most. At some level, he believes that these are the people least likely to reject him. He has an extraordinary degree of insecurity. He was likely raised in an environment where authentic and consistent expression of healthy emotion was absent or unacceptable. His perception of self, confirmed over the course of his life, has caused him to feel empty and "less than" for no apparent reason. We typically call his perception of self to be "shame based."

He copes with his underlying shame by pushing it out of his mind. He doesn't know how to address feelings too big for him to grasp. So he has no resolve, no emotional growth. He spends his life trying to prove to himself and others that he isn't what his deepest self-image says that he is...a nothing.

He needs validation from others because he is convinced that he cannot get it from himself. He judges himself by what he does rather than who he perceives himself to be. He has convinced himself over a lifetime that his shame-based emotions are to be masked and protected at any cost. And he does a wonderful job of this outside the home.

But close personal relationships are based on the very emotions he protects. Therefore, anyone trying to connect with these emotions becomes the enemy. His reliance on performance and ability to measure success doesn't work at home. At home, he is expected to be "himself." But as described throughout this book, his deepest feelings are in a place neither he nor anyone else is allowed to go. So when those closest to him look for connection, his defenses go up in the form of anger. And the closer the relationship the more threat it poses.

My personal experience working with the angry man has convinced me that his angry behavior is in direct proportion to his feelings of shame. He is always running from his shame. And because he didn't (or wasn't able to) address these difficult feelings as a child, he is unaware they are even there.

The bottom line: If he doesn't talk it out, he'll act it out, whether he is aware of it or not. This is his lifelong experience. Shame is his nemesis and he feels he must always be on guard.

Why do men and women seem to handle anger differently?

If you think about how youngsters play, little boys still play with toys like army men. Their interaction with the army men is mostly singular. The army men have a mission, a direction, and they're non-emotional. And army men don't communicate with each other. They are more cognitive in nature, and they're self-directed, as well.

On the other hand, girls play with dolls, right? Well, what do the dolls do? They have tea parties and relationships and talk and chat. They communicate with each other. So while young girls find that being a successful female in society is to have good relationships, young boys learn that to be a successful man is to be independent, unemotional, and able to stand on his own.

The result of this upbringing or "programming" is that men are not given an effective outlet for resolving conflict or emotional pain, whereas women are trained from infancy to rely on relationships and to develop their communication, giving them extensive options for dealing with difficulty. So, for many men, the Anger Shield becomes their most trusted tool early on in life.

Why do some men always have to be right or always have to prove their point?

Angry men live in the cognitive zone. When there is a dispute or argument it's rarely about what's right or wrong for him. It just appears this way. The angry man is unable to remove his mask and lower his shield. For him to be wrong about something is to be wrong as a person. So he remains in the cognitive zone, which is about logic, right and wrong, and quantitative value.

In relationships, logic and cognition are largely irrelevant. Relationships require emotion in order to be successful. So the best he can do is win, which is justifying to himself that his position is right. For the angry man, that's about as happy as he gets.

This is also why angry men can have a difficult time with being apologetic. When an angry man is working on a cognitive level, not in touch with his emotions, saying he's sorry is apologizing for not being wrong. To say he's sorry is to open up an emotional gate. And it doesn't make sense to him to say he's sorry for being right.

I often ask the men I work with, "Do you want to be right or do you want to be happy?" I point out to them that being right is based on logic and cognition, while being happy is an emotional process.

How can I tell if he really has an anger problem, or it's just me being selfish?

That's a great question. Because a lot of times, a significant other such as a wife or girlfriend, or even a child or a mom, will look at him and tell him that he has an anger problem. But he often won't acknowledge it, other than admitting that he blows up "once in awhile." He can't figure it out yet because his psyche isn't ready for him to accept that this problem is his and his responsibility to fix. To admit it would mean that he's hurt so many people without justification. He often isn't ready to admit this to himself until calamity strikes (divorce, arrests, job loss).

I ask men struggling with anger to honestly ask themselves the questions listed earlier in this book. If they are honest and answer yes to at least two of them, it is likely that they have a problem with anger. This has been my experience working with angry men.

Why do angry men insist on doing everything their way and get furious when you offer help or suggestions?

The angry man has an extreme need or expectation

for feeling autonomous, or independent. Their desire for autonomy tells them that they don't have permission to "not know" or to say "I don't know how" or "I need some help."

But in reality, because they cannot possibly fix everything around them, and because they're not working on themselves and are so caught up in doing things right, they are actually very dependent on things needing to go the way they need them to go.

It's ironic, because what they really want is to be independent, but instead they find themselves dependent on the rest of the world to do exactly what they need. For example, if a spouse is having a good day, the angry man in his self-centered wisdom will say: Wow, she must really be happy with me and what I'm doing today because look at her, she's thrilled. He thinks it's all about him. He's the center of her and everyone's life.

When she has a great day, then he feels as if he won. On the other hand, when she has a bad day, he feels inside, without realizing it, that he has failed. He asks himself: What did I do wrong? And he projects onto her his feeling of failure. He has a distorted perception, that she is accusing him of ruining her day. That's not what's happening at all, but that's the nature of the anger cycle and the angry man. That's needing someone else on the outside to fill his emptiness on the inside. So that's why if things go wrong, it's doubly upsetting. It's not just that something went wrong, but something went wrong that has taken away his control of his environment, another person, or situation.

How do you know when it's time to seek professional help?

I think with any sort of problem, the time to seek professional help is when one makes the decision or realization that whatever is going on is putting obstacles in their life that are blocking their ability to be happy. The problem for angry men is that they've never been happy. So their definition of happiness is not what you, and now me, experience. Their only definition of happiness is being right.

They realize they're unhappy, but they determine that something outside of them needs to change in order to become happy. So they will remove themselves from a situation. They will get a new job. They will find new friends. They will get a new car. Get a new wife. They'll do whatever seems right. If one grows up believing that their environment has all the power over their sense of value and sense of self, then if they don't like it, they are simply going to try to recreate the environment. For you and me, if we understand that we are not happy, rather than look to recreate the environment, we look inside and try to recreate or make changes in ourselves. The angry man is more caught up in what happens rather than how to deal with what happens.

The majority of referrals come to me through wives or girlfriends. And there's good reason for this: there's a cycle that takes place. There are reasons that women will hook up with angry men. They're looking for the same affirmation; they're just doing it in two different ways.

When the angry man is looking for affirmation, he does his little dance, his manipulation, whatever he needs to do in order to impress Susie-Q. Susie, at the same time, looks past the manipulation and likes how she feels. She looks at what he's giving her rather than how she's really feeling. She's empty as well. So she finds somebody who is giving her a sense of attention that makes her feel like she's okay. So Susie's getting what she needs from him. He's being adored by her. And while all couples, healthy couples, have this, the difference is that the two of them are lacking a sense of value of self and self-esteem. They are looking at each other to fill that need. And that's why there is such extreme connection and enmeshment, as we call it. They both lack the ability to date slowly or carefully. These relationships usually come together very quickly because each party has, in their mind, found the answer to their problems.

Well, what happens? They get together and norms set in. And one day Joe comes home and is no longer able to put on his act. He starts being the old Joe—the one lacking a sense of value inside. He becomes angry as a defense so that Susie can't see how inadequate he really feels.

And then Susie isn't getting what she needs because he's not manipulating her to make her feel better. Susie is looking for him to be okay because then she can be okay. And when she's not feeling okay, she tries to do more of what she would normally do, which might be dote over him or adore him. But he's busy keeping her out because he's feeling threatened that she's going to see, or already sees, how empty he really feels inside. And he doesn't even realize he feels empty. He'll project this feeling of emptiness by making his feelings her fault:

she's not enough, or the job's not enough. And again, he externalizes in order to compensate for the degree of emptiness he feels inside. It's like a teeter-totter. He's trying to get that balance back.

The lower he feels, the more he's going to defend with the anger shield. He has suppressed his true feelings for so long that he doesn't even know that he's feeling it. All that he knows is that he's angry. And he has to have a reason, so she becomes the reason, because now she is not meeting his need to feel better. He doesn't realize it, but he's the only one who can make himself feel better. He's in a place where he's not accepting something. He's in a place where he's got resentments that have built up. He's feeling insecurities that he doesn't even know exists. He's feeling ostracized, maybe insecure about his relationship with her. He's feeling that he's not good enough for her. So he projects his feelings and believes that she's thinking that she's better than he, when in fact, she's just hoping he'd had a nice day.

So it all comes down to this: When you see things going wrong in your life that are preventing happiness, and you don't understand what to do, it's probably time to get some professional help.

Why do I get so caught up in fixing the relationship and making him happy—even when I know it's him that has the problem?

You're doing the same thing he's doing. You're trying to fix him so that you can feel better and keep the relationship. The fact is, what we really need to do is say: What do I need in this situation? What is most important?

If I am most important, even more than my relationship, what do I need in order to take care of myself? Well, if I need him to act respectfully, then I can communicate that. But somewhere in the near future I need to have a cut-off point, a plan, like: "Joe, if you continue this one more time, I am going to..." whether it be going to the other room or leaving the relationship; whatever it needs to be.

If things are getting kind of stressed and he's getting upset, it's important to pick your battles so that you can win the war.

And winning the war is not fixing him. It's doing what's best for you (and your children).

Remember that the anger he shows is a shield. Respect the shield and move out of the way as long as you're not being personally attacked. Then, when you see him getting irritable or discontent over what seems like nothing, know that he is needing space away from feeling vulnerable, whether it be his saying to himself "I'm not good enough," or "I'm failing again," or "I hate the world," whatever the case may be. The last thing we want to do at that moment is try to connect with him.

What he's trying to do at that moment is gain control of his environment. He's never going to truly gain the control, but it doesn't help you at all when you are trying so hard to connect emotionally and he's trying so hard to not connect emotionally.

Often, for women who are very verbal, the most difficult thing to do is to walk away and give him his space.

And it's ironic, because we angry men tend to be very articulate, usually above average in intelligence, and hardworking. Our tongue—our articulation—is a weapon we use to keep people away. It also gets us what we want.

And he fails to realize that she's coming from an emotional place. The angry man will say, "If I can just explain it right and just show her the logic, then she'll understand why I'm right. And she'll be fine with it and she'll understand me." Just because he's verbal doesn't mean he's getting to a feeling level.

So look at the extremes. When the angry man experiences some sort of threat or fear, he goes cognitive. When the woman experiences threat or fear, she goes emotional.

The disjoint comes when there's an extreme on both ends. In general, she leaves her head behind and goes straight to the emotion. And he leaves any sense of feeling behind and goes to his cognitive thinking.

The vast majority of men that I see come to me as a result of a crisis: a blow-up or something else that happened, whether it be an assault, or domestic violence, or a wife saying, "I'm going to divorce you," or whatever the case may be. Usually, someone mentions that they better get some professional assistance or else, so they come to the conclusion that they need it, real quick!

Ultimately, though, the angry men are the ones who have to come to that conclusion on their own, because nobody can fix this for them, even though this is what they have depended on their entire lives.

FINAL THOUGHTS

IF we look at the angry man as one who is dependent on another to act the way he needs them to so that he'll feel okay, then we can see what happens when that someone falls short. The angry man's need for validation becomes threatened. He tends to feel like a victim without even knowing it. He conjured up an unreasonable expectation, that if so-and-so would have just acted this way or that, then he would have felt okay.

I did this myself. I grew up with a father who essentially blamed me for almost everything, and I learned very young that making him happy was my role if I wanted affirmation. I felt value only when I could see that I was making him happy. Back then, I didn't realize that I couldn't make him happy, and that he was unhappy through no fault of my own. As a result, I spent most of my life looking for affirmation from my father without even realizing it. Though I rebelled many times, I still held on to a longing for my father's affirmation. I never got it before he died.

As I grew older, I emulated his emotional dependence through expectations. I could only be happy if things went in such a way that I received affirmation that I was okay. Back then, I didn't know that it was my job to make me happy. I thought it was my job to take care of your feelings and your job to take care of mine. I've learned that I was wrong on both counts.

Expectations for purposes of self-esteem are a setup for misery. The irony is that the angry man's goal of autonomy and independence is actually the converse. In reality, the angry man lives emotionally dependent on others to determine his self-worth. It has never occurred to him that he can find validation and respect within himself. But as he was taught early on, his feelings didn't matter. His value had to come from someone or something else.

Angry guys almost always feel unique. They also feel very alone. And even though others have suggestions and solutions, and try to help him, our angry man says, "Those solutions won't work for me because I'm different." So they have no one but themselves to get answers from or from which to find happiness. If people don't do as they want, they try to manipulate. If that doesn't work, they turn to anger. He does what he needs to feel in control— even if it's at the expense of those who love him.

But in reality all they ever get is thinking that they won...that they proved they were right. Sadly, they can never be happy this way.

I am grateful that I've changed. I hope that other men will learn through my experience. They and their families deserve better.

About the Author

Evan Katz, M.C., LPC is fondly known as "The Anger Guy." Counseling angry men and teens since 1994, his expertise is amongst the best in his field. What makes him stand out is that he's lived it. He tells his story of life as an angry man; not changing until after his father's unexpected death. He maintained a full-time private practice in the Atlanta area until July 2010, when he was diagnosed with late stage cancer. Today, he speaks professionally to colleagues, companies, and communities; addressing the most unhealthy social epidemic amongst men and boys throughout the Western world—ANGER!

CPSIA information can be obtained
at www.ICGtesting.com
Printed in the USA
LVOW07s0505051017
551257LV00024B/224/P